Bhopal Gas Tragedy

Poetry Across Nature, Life and Miseries

R. P. Ghosh

BlueRose ONE
Stories Matter

First Published in December 2022

ISBN: 978-93-5668-554-3

BLUEROSE PUBLISHERS

www.BlueRoseONE.com

info@bluerosepublishers.com

+91 8882 898 898

Cover Design:

R.P.Ghosh

Typographic Design:

Namrata Saini

Distributed by: BlueRose, Amazon, Flipkart

About the Author

Rudrendra Prasad Ghosh, (born:16th November 1944–), popularly known as R.P. Ghosh, is simultaneously recognized as an author, painter, poet, sculptor, and a nature lover. To pursue his inherent passion for art and literature; he took early voluntary retirement from a secured and dignified service as 'General Manager' of an undertaking, functioning under the Ministry of Commerce, Government of India, in 2001.

Born on 16th November 1944, at 'Narail', a suburb town of 'Jessore' district (now in Bangladesh) of undivided India, he became, at an early age, along with his parents and relatives, a refugee, as a victim of the political turmoil which caused the partition of his homeland, while forming two sovereign nations - India and Pakistan in 1947.

Crossing the border between the newly formed nations, his parents and relatives took shelter in a refugee camp and went from there to a resettlement town at 'Habra' of District North 24- Parganas, near Calcutta (now Kolkata) in independent India.

He obtained his school education initially from local schools, and also from Ramakrishna Mission Vidyapith (Dist: Purulia, West Bengal, India), a chain of educational institutions, being run under philosophic guidance, formulated by Swami Vivekananda, the great philosopher, social- reformer and pioneer of the Indian Renaissance. Thereafter; he graduated from the Art faculty of the Government College of Art, Calcutta in 1968, and started his initial service career in the advertising profession.

He joined 'Nehru Science Centre', under the Ministry of Education and Culture, Government of India, in 1976 at Mumbai. And in 1983, he joined a leading Corporation, under the Ministry of Commerce, Government of India, at New Delhi.

During his long public service career, he visited several countries, i.e. the United Kingdom, France, Soviet Russia (USSR), Germany (FRG & GDR), Egypt, the UAE and many other countries in the Middle East, number of times.

His creative talents in art and literature reflect his own style of expression, elaborating wide exposures, experiences and interactions with a cross section of people in societies from different countries and times.

Apart from his drawings, paintings and sculptures, in the literary area, he has authored twelve titles to date. These also include collections of poems and stories in both English and Bengali language.

Also by the Author

'Podatik' (Pedestrian) - Collection of Bengali Short-Stories, written by the author, based on his experiences and interactions with people in India and abroad, time to time. Published in April, 2003.

'Eklavyer Noibedya' (Offerings of 'Eklavya') - Collection of Bengali Poems. Published in April, 2003.

'Sukh-Sagorer Khonj' (Search for Eternal Enlightenment) - Collection of Bengali Poems. Published in April, 2003.

'Beedehir Roop' (Beauty of the Bodiless) - Collection of Bengali Poems. Published in August, 2006.

'Lunchita Sokuntola' (Humiliated 'Sokuntola') - Bengali Poem of one-act play, referring to 'Sakuntala' of an Indian-epic on the theme against women's oppression in human-society. Published in January, 2010.

'Mondakinir Achena Pakhi' (Unknown bird of 'Mondakini') - Collection of Bengali Poems. Published in August, 2010. (By 'Prativash', Kolkata, India.)

'Basonter Vorbela' (Morning of the Spring) - Collection of - Bengali Poems. Published in January, 2013. (By Saptarshi Prakashan, Kolkata, India.) ISBN: 9789382706335.

'Poetry Collection... And The Modhumoti Flows Quietly' – Collection of English Poems. Published in June, 2016. (By Olympia Publishers, London.) ISBN: 987-1-84897-689-4.

'The Treasure Of Tears' – Collection of English Poems. Published in May, 2018. (By Olympia Publishers, London.) ISBN: 978-1-78830-085-8.

'Polasher Rupokar' (Creator of 'Polash' flower, the flame of the forest) – Collection of Bengali Poems. Published in October, 2018. (By Saptarshi Prakashan, Kolkata, India.) ISBN: 9789387158641.

'Beloved Oblivion"– Collection of English Poems. Published in September, 2020. (By Olympia Publishers, London.) ISBN: 978-1-78830-494-8.

'BAPU- in My Dream'– Collection of English Poems. Published in September, 2022. (By Notion Press Media Private Limited, Chennai, India.) ISBN: 979-8-88805-372-0.

Dedication

In memory of those more than a thousand victims,
who lost their innocent lives in a disaster due to leakage of
lethal methyl isocyanate (MIC) gas from a pesticide plant
in Bhopal of India on the night of 3rd December 1984,
and to express solidarity with thousands of
sufferers maimed lifelong thereafter.

Acknowledgments

Life and Nature have always acted on me as boons of fortune. Forever, I am grateful for their abundant blessings. Apart from their almightiness, I feel lucky to have a wide circle of patrons, readers, and well-wishers, who remember me regularly, honour and review my creative and literary talents and outputs, thereby encouraging my efforts, in a positive mood, to guide me with the right perspective all the time.

Further, I am always eager to receive the comments, criticisms and reactions of the readers, and poetry-lovers, as I believe, these will definitely pave me the direction towards perfection.

As ever; I am grateful to the entire team of Blue Rose Publishers, who have extended their wholehearted generosity and support to publish this Poetry book, thereby, providing me with an opportunity to reach towards a wider spectrum of readers, reviewers, critics and patrons as well, beyond my expectations, crossing the borders and barriers.

I gratefully acknowledge the support and assistance of the media, as well.

My thanks to everyone, who is involved in the process of marketing the book in wide circle, directly or indirectly.

Truly yours,
R. P. Ghosh.

Date: 08th September , 2022.
Mobile & WhatsApp: +91 9871168861.
Kolkata -700009, India.
Email: ghoshr77@yahoo.in

Contents

Fairy-February beacons the Spring

Crossing over a long spell of Winter season,
all admirers of the vast Nature have assembled
to attend the crowning-ceremony of the 'Spring',
on an early February morning.
Elegantly dressed in bright sap-green feathers,
the flocks of Parrots are gladly taking part
in musical concert on the branches of a tree.
Cuckoo has yet to attend the concert as an invitee.

A few Parrots perhaps have already noticed
my absence in this pleasant occasion
that is being arranged after a long gap of interval,
beyond the rainy season.
Some of them have straightway flew up
to my cottage and peeped-in through the window
to wake me up from my morning prayer.
Delightfully, I welcome them into the garden.

Parrots know the consequences–
The pale-brown and dry leaves are almost ready
to say good-bye to the beloved Nature.
To fill-up the gap, the tender-leaves will appear
on every stalk of the branches in near future.
With a great hope, I feel myself delighted–
The trees will regain their desired green-beauty.
The flocks of birds will get-back their usual

charming musical tunes in different rhythms.
The birds will again nidify their nests on these
green foliage to welcome new life in the Nature.

Meanwhile; I am delighted to get humming-notes
of the bees, flying around the peduncles
of cheerful mango-plants, while spreading over
exciting essence in the air to invite butterflies.
Plants of seasonal flowers are busy in budding-spree.
The butterflies are not lagging behind;
spreading the wings, they are flying in their usual
competitive-mood among each other, to be familiar
with colourful flowers to taste hidden honey-drops,
also to ensure pollination, as early as possible.

I am spell-bound to witness the panoramic elevation
of all seven colours on budding petals of flowers,
combined with seven musical-notes in the tunes
of the bees and birds on this splendid occasion
that is being arranged by the great Nature,
to welcome Spring, the king of all seasons.

02nd February, 2016.

Tale of a Tiny Pebble

One small town had already been created
by the affectionate care of the hills all around.
I have received a call to attend a function there.
To turn-down all the speculations; the cloud
conveyed the information on early arrival of rains.
The greenery around the town mostly remain busy
with their childhood playmates, the hilly rocks.

I am an unknown face to all of them.
The shy hillocks cover themselves under the veils
of flying clouds, like the newly married brides.
On the event of their meeting together; perhaps
my presence is not solicited by none of them.
Even the raindrops are jealous of me; as I am
an unwanted guest on this private holy event.
After all; hills, greenery, cloud and rain-drops
are members of the same family of the Nature.

Timely the cloud bursts into raindrops.
Current of rainwater flows the subterranean stream.
The pebbles of different shapes, who have, so far,
been accompanying the clouds and the rain-drops
from hilly tops, are now abandoned, and left alone
along the banks by the current of restless stream
who is eager to flow down to meet the river.

The elegant colours, shapes and sizes of the pebbles
attract my eyes, thereby, I pick-up a few of them
from the damp and wet land along the bank.
I find; the shining tiny pebble has already recorded
a tale of her long journey detailing all pleasant and

humiliations on her shining surface, including her
annoyances against the cloud and raindrops,
along with the soil, her childhood inmates.

Happily they started their journey, and very shortly
met a new playmate namely the stream.
Initially the stream was very gentle, cool and calm.
But the grown-up cloud in multiple volume, and
the rain inspired the stream to become restless
and asked her to flow in rapid force.
While rolling with her; I was gradually changing
my attitude, and comparatively I became polished
and smother to maintain the space along with them.

Dear pedestrian! Very soon the stream transformed
her youth into a vibrant river; swelling up the banks.
And she didn't care for me any further and left alone.
One by one; I was also deserted by all my playmates.

Please do not repeat the same precedence as they did
to me along with other pebbles; even at odd moment.
Instead; let us take the oath to create a new milestone
of modern human settlement by forming a township
homogeneous to the Nature on the riverbank,
as once upon a time, Mohenjo-Daro, Harappa
and Mesopotamia were created, as notable mark
of ancient history of human civilization in the world.
Listening to this tale, I feel myself inspired and kiss
the tiny pebble for having a noble heart and mind.

05th February, 2016.
(In memory of my visit to Phuntsholing
of Bhutan, while crossing the river 'Torsa', in 1999.)

The Death-Warrant

Your Majesty, the Lord of 'Death'!
I beg to present my humble submission—
Even on receiving your warrant,
my absence to your majestic court was not
a deliberate attempt on my part.
I know; it has, no doubt, annoyed your mind
against me and my behaviour.
Therefore I believe; as violation of an order,
obviously I shall be convicted for committing
an offence of 'contempt of court'.

Oh the Lord of 'Death'!
Very well you know; nobody has ever dared
to ignore your warrant, and I am not an exception.
Honestly speaking; without the knowledge
of anyone of my near-n-dear, in an early morning,
in presence of tender Sun, leaving my body behind,
I left my residence for an undisclosed destination.
It was the hope that; my mind, as directed by soul,
could reach your court well in time.

For your kind information;
I had with me only the warrant, and nothing else.
Not the warrant had any mention of any
individual's name, who was addressed to
and the proper address even.

Further, the warrant did not clarify the direction
of destination and whom I am supposed to report to.

Oh the Lord of 'Death'!
I know very well, no one has so far even
dared to dishonour your warrant.
I swear, I had no intention to be disobedient.
Followings are my affidavit in advance
for your kind consideration—
As soon as I received your summon;
in order to obey your instruction, immediately
even without anyone's knowledge, I abandoned
all my lovely attachments forever.
My body seized the flow of blood-circulation
and the pulse-rate as well.
My brain refused to function and went on 'Coma',
only to respond to your final call of ultimatum.

But the gracious and affectionate touch
of kind hearted Earth and the vast Nature
stood coherently on my way.
Nevertheless; all my relatives and well-wishers
through their whole-hearted efforts
provided me the best possible medical care
and tried hard to divert the route of destination.
Their day-n-night nursing ultimately revived me
and dragged me back to their clutch again.

Oh my Lord! I didn't even know; whether
you became pleased to their tireless efforts,
or, they had your blessings in disguise.

Day-by-day; I forgot to fulfill all my commitments
that, I had already made before you.
Thereby; I failed to obey the holy appointment, that
had already been granted to me by your kind court.
Not even my body, heart and mind did not like
to be parted with their beloved soul.
Their long attachments and association with the soul
created main hindrance to get your gracious presence.
The soul; leaving aside the mundane attachments
of my body-heart and mind, even refused
to proceed further towards your majestic court.

In fact; I did not possess the credibility like that of
holy-boy 'Nachiketa' who, in his living human-form,
could directly meet you at your court, as mentioned
in age-old reference of Hindu epic—'Upanishad'.
Ultimately I failed to avail this rare and holy
opportunity of achieving credibility to meet
your gracious presence timely, and pay due respect.
As a result; the sentry on duty at the main gate
of your official-court did not permit me to get in.
Hence; I had no other alternative but to return
to the same address of my residence on the Earth.

Your Majesty!
However; going through these consequences,
my mind bears breeds of doubts, one after another.
For ages the proverb prevails in the Earth that, never
you get a wrong identity of an individual to call for.
There might be an apprehension of creating
deliberate confusion in the mind of your assistants

who were deputed to deliver the same warrant
to the proper and right addressee.
Perhaps they had confusion about dual identification
of the addressee, as duplication of same name
was quite possible in overpopulated human society
on any part of this Earth.

Perhaps by mistake; the warrant was delivered
at the wrong address, as facial similarity and
identical appearance between two men are not
out of question and not even impossible at all.
As a result; I lost the chance of fulfilling my most
important achievement, which is the ultimate and
universal desire of every human beings.

My Lord! We all know; you are the Supreme
in the universal and the vast 'Death' kingdom.
If you do not get anyone else to assist you
in discharging such massive activities worldwide;
and you are managing whole cycles yourself alone,
perhaps, you are to be blamed for these lapses.
Ultimately; I am the beneficiary of these lapses
as I have gained an extra mileage of longevity.
All my relatives, near-n-dears and well-wishers
are happy and highly delighted.
But; I deeply console to the tragic demise of that
unknown soul, who has lost the life unwillingly
to bear the compensation of your mishandling.
I do not even know his or her name and address.

My dear Lord of 'Death'!
Perhaps; you might remember the tragic incident
that I had to bear during my youth, as and when,
my dearest expired at her young age all of a sudden.
By virtue of your greatness; you know very well
the exact timing, whom to call and when.
At the time of final call; you welcome all life-beings
to your affectionate arms without any disparity.
At the same time, you punish the offenders impartially.
But does anyone dare to penalize you for the lapses
you have already committed; as happened in my case?
Obviously; I'll try to get the answer to this question
from you; as and when I receive subsequent warrant
to be issued to me next time from your good offices.

Hope; with your virtual greatness; you will pardon
my audacity for addressing this question.
And at that moment, it will be my pleasure
to dedicate this poem on your multiple honour.

08th February, 2016.

(My feelings after recovery from 'Coma', following the neurological surgery in my brain, to treat acute subdual hematoma over cerebral convexity due to an accident.)

Tang of the Trio

We, the three –
Body, Heart and Mind, always claim
the combined credit of bringing-up and
manifest the aspiration of every life-being
into totality on this vast earthy surface.
We, the three, follow multiple activities–
comprising of the both, good and bad.
But; to claim credit, always we remain
engaged in comparing the superiority
among ourselves.

From the very first moment
of our appearance on this earth, we, three,
are living together and active enough
to focus on our vibrant existences
in placements, which we had inherited
from the unknown sources.

We pretend to be very powerful and
united to the outer world and onlookers.
But it is not the fact always.
We combine our strength, as and when
we jointly decide to take part for some
praiseworthy acts, or to commit crimes,
and offences harmful to others.
After committing the nuisance;

as and when we take rest in comfort,
silently we raise the points to identify–
who is the main culprit and responsible,
while conducting the offence.
Without proper retrospection and analysis;
straightway we pinpoint our fingers
to accuse each others, but no one is willing
to share responsibility.
Even after placing all important arguments,
we exert ourselves to prove each one
as noble and innocent.

On the contrast;
while doing some commendable and
praiseworthy activities, each one of us
prominently express our sincere willingness
to grab all the credits,
leaving aside the sense of equality
and rational feelings, altogether.

In general, we, the Trio –
retain differences of opinions, thereby create
tensions in the matter of serious concerns.
To dissolve these issues;
very often we jointly proceed
towards different holy destinations
of the pilgrimages at Temples, Churches,
Mosques, Pagodas and Gurdwaras
at different locations.
But; no priest of any faiths has, so far,
been able to solve our differences and

to bring us to an amicable settlement.
Finally; as and when we breath our last
in this Earth, it is decided to hand over
all the disputes to the great–'Time'.

Apart from all these; main issue of our
differences is about the sovereignty,
and the 'Supremacy' on all the life-beings.
It is yet to be decided, among ourselves,
who is the Supreme-in-Command.
Till date, the dispute is not yet settled.

On funny behaviour;
either from the Heart or the Mind,
sometimes I, the Body, feel myself irritated
and do not even hesitate to express
my honest reaction,
– Please take a note minutely.
  Without my support and tolerance,
  your very existence remains in stake.
  In the form of human body, I have
  lifelong given you comfortable shelter
  and noble support always.
  Therefore; to establish your generosity,
  please be obliged to me.
  Hope you will agree; you do not have
  any separate identity, or, any individual
  existence without my presence.
  Nevertheless; as a 'Body', I am the
  supreme among ourselves, all the three.

Now; to oppose the arguments of the Body,
both the Heart and Mind present their views
confidently and reply gently,
– Dear! Without our presence and
  active participation, you are lifeless.
  As a body; you are static, or just like
  any other perishable object, without having
  any living identity.
  We know the mastery and tricks–
  how to play the strings of life to create
  the tune of melody, as well as the tragedy.
  We are the custodians to regulate
  the treasury of joy and pleasure,
  weal and woes, sorrows and tears
  in everybody's life.

For a while; as Body, I feel myself
cornered and humiliated.
Thereafter; to teach them a lesson
about overall perspective of the life
in the vast nature, categorically
I remind them about holy presence
of the 'Soul', who is always guiding
both of them, from behind.
Now; both the Heart and Mind jointly
submit their observations confidently,
– Dear Body! These are all rubbish!
  You are living in a flimsy paradise.
  'Soul' is solely dependent on us –
  the 'Trio', Body-Heart and Mind.

Without the existence of us, the 'Trio',
'Soul' is absolutely an abstract concept
of all human-beings.
An ideological and debatable confusion
have been carried on for ages; without
having any link with the reality of life.
Human-beings; very often, talk about
attainment of salvation of their 'Soul',
after their last breath on this Earth.
If the human-beings, at all, believe
in the faith of achieving salvation
of their 'Soul', they may please be
advised to participate sincerely in
welfare activities selflessly for the
common people of their society
during their lifetime, without expecting
any kind of benefit in return, at any time.

Having following this practice
during their lifetime, their 'Soul' will
automatically attain ultimate salvation.

12th February, 2016.

Apple-Tree of the 'Eden'

On your eyelashes, always I find
the mystic hints that of 'Eve' of Biblical-Epic.
On your lip-movement I feel seductive vent
of your hidden heart and mind.
As if; I am alone in the green 'Eden' garden.
And I get myself confused; what is to be done.

It seems; I am the same man 'Adam'–
seduced by Satan, and you are that woman,
'Eve', driven out from the heaven.

You desire for a love-tryst to meet me alone
and standing under the same Apple-tree.
But you feel scared and terrified by the presence
of a poisonous snake, moving hood for biting.
So that; you bear the afflictions lifelong.

Since then; both of us, like 'Adam' and 'Eve'
started our long journey, without having
proper direction and avenue of final destination.
And the passage was full of rubbles and hurdles.
The rough and zigzag road is still going ahead.

Meanwhile; with your power of vision, you
enlightened my heart and mind in right direction–
Love is painful like the poisonous snake-bite.
Yet; without love, the journey in life is incomplete.
Love directs the life to overcome all the hurdles
and paves the path towards the holy godliness.

15th February, 2016.

My Faith On His Eternal-Truth

Since my childhood; my mother taught me
the manners to touch the feet of my elders,
while paying respect to them on holy occasions.
Till today; with all my sincerity, I follow
the same practice.

My dear Mom!
With this realization; during my journey in life,
it is my humble submission to you–
While blessing; please do not advise me,
either to embrace, or to be baptized to any
individual religious-faith.
Rather; guide me towards the right direction,
how to proceed towards the truth of eternity
of the Almighty, who is, in disguise, regularly
governing the solar system in this Universe.
Even; directing all seasons about the routine –
when to appear in this Earth, and when to depart.

Teach me right rituals and proper lessons;
how to enlighten myself with his blessings.
I austerely desire to dedicate myself to his
ideology, which is manifested everywhere,
even in every nook-n-corner on this Earth.

Mom! Please advise me –
How an individual religious ideology does

really matter to a human mind ultimately!
Is it not merely the repetition of same idea;
drafted in different scripts and languages
by different personalities in different modes
at different time and social frames?

Instead of promoting one united society
with strong bond of unity of greater humanity;
ultimately, indulging in dividing the society
in many sections, in order to protect and
exaggerate of an individual's personal image
and interest through his or her disciples–
By this process; can we attain blessings
from the Almighty?
Or, can we attain ultimate salvation?

Following this process, can we overpower
and subdue the inherent six-vices, which are
already existing in our body and mind?
Can we follow the process of self-purification?

The scarf of a religious-priest is colourful
and nicely designed with different holy-scripts
in different languages.
Those wordings and verses do not inspire me
to purify my mind and soul any more.
My starving mind is always in search of
the great Creator and supreme Regulator.
Guide me please, how to get his blessings!

03rd March, 2016. New Delhi, India.

Homage to 'Khuswant'

Oh my dear 'Lord of Death'!
Couldn't you grant him at least a year more
to the length of his longevity to score
and mark a Century on this Earth?
Perhaps; you might be feeling bore
in absence of the witty jokes of our
dear and loving 'Khushwant' in your
elegant and illustrious court, for last
many years, as his masterly stokes
repeatedly delighted and enlightened us
in order to energize our mind and soul
during all these years.
Very well you knew; we were lucky enough
and 'khus-kismat' to live on this Earth,
where your Highness allowed 'Khushwant'
to take the birth.
Those neighbours of the place 'Khushab',
a district town, now in Pakistan,
were feeling themselves embarrassed
with old memories of that naughty boy:
'Khushwant'!
Probably his childhood attachment lately
inspired that grown-up boy to pen-down
a memorable novel 'Train To Pakistan'.

Indeed; that novel, reminds me today even
the horrible events of communal riots
and brutal killings of innocent people
that ultimately forced me in my childhood
to flee at midnight, through a river-route,
leaving behind the birth place of mine
and my ancestors for generations, then
crossing the temporary boundary of a country
newly formed, East-Pakistan, that was created
bifurcating union of India— the original land.
Oh Khushwant! Ultimately you are lucky
to find a permanent address, but I am not.
Rather; I am passing a continuous journey
from one place to another today even,
and living like a refugee, without identity.

20th March, 2016. New Delhi.

In memory of Late Khushwant Singh, (Feb,1915–20th Mar, 2014) a leading author, lawyer, diplomat and journalist of India.

Bird 'Koel' wails in early Summer

The season 'Spring' has just been over.
In early morning; while flying from branch
to branch, the estranged bird 'koel' goes on
singing in her heart-breaking and touchy
musical notations.
Nobody knows; what she desires to convey
and what she is looking for between leaves
and the branches, in early Summer season.

My sympathetic and curious mind
tries to find out the reason–
Perhaps; the bird Cuckoo is looking for
the particular nest, nidificated by other bird,
where she secretly laid her eggs, without
anyone's knowledge, during her last
breeding cycle, nearly a year back.
Further; my mind is eager to confirm,
whether she has been able to find out
whereabouts and well-beings of her
affectionate and beloved chicks!

I feel for a moment, perhaps these are my
superfluous thoughts.
Rather; she is keen to know the welfare of
all human beings, including their near-n-dear
in the society, after a gap of nearly a year.

I feel myself confused, what I shall reply!
The part of precious treasure that was
handed over to me as custodian, and I was
advised to protect and preserve them properly.
But unfortunately; due to my inefficiency
and negligence, those have been grossly
misappropriated within a year, part by part.

In the evening; my mind feels frustrated,
since there is neither much time left, nor
even a single beam of sunlight is in sight
to formulate and discharge the duties.
On retrospection; my mind tries to find out
the fact that, in the past, by virtue of my
selfish attitude, I had already consumed
and manipulated sizable volume of precious
natural resources without proper justification.
But so far; neither I have been accounted for
on single occasion, nor, I have been able
to return even a single farthing.

The Spring has just been over; and Summer,
the first season of new cycle, is just on arrival.
The heaps of dried leaves are ungracefully
scattered on the ground, hither-n-thither
and are being carried away by the harsh wind,
thereby, creating melodious rustles.
The sound-reflections of the rustles are

probably being rehearsed by the wailing 'koel'
as her message on farewell, in musical tune
to all human-beings in this vast Nature.

16th April, 2016. Rohini, New Delhi.
Bird 'Cuckoo' is known as 'Koel' and
'Kokil' in Southi-East Asian Countries.

Summery-feelings of 'Gitanjali'

On this holy Summer festival–
I am unable to offer red petals of 'May-flowers'.
Even, bloomed red-Oleander is in shabby status.
The cuckoos are also reluctant
to join the musical concert on this yearly event.

The situation sprouts inferiority complex
in my mind, and the questionnaire crumbles
my depressed mind, one after another–
Do we possess the credibility, or, are we really
eligible to celebrate the memorable occasion
on 8th May, birth anniversary of one great poet
and humanist, the world has ever seen?

'Tagore', the great Poet!
Every line of your lyrics resonates the feelings
of amity and universal brotherhood.
Lifelong you were the follower and propagator
of this esteemed ideology.
Always you had kept yourself far away
from conservativeness and superstations,
like a bird flying high in the boundless sky.
The blackened cloud and cyclonic storm
could not dare to distract and divert your mind
from devotion and sincerity.

The fact is already recorded as reference –

You had spent enumerable sleepless nights
due to the reasons of various social and political
disturbances, which cropped-up from the clashes
and bloodsheds, initiated by power-crazy people
having vested interests with narrow objectives
of controlling and ruling over the masses
worldwide, even during your life time.
As instance; First-world-war was one of them,
when humanity was disrupted ruthlessly.

'Tagore', the Humanist!
World-scenario, today even, is in volatile state
as the political-magnets of so-called developed
countries are eager to formulate new principle
of judgment and to set different 'world-order'.
Nevertheless; they are also engaging themselves
in controversy to decide on an important point–
'Who would exercise the power of sovereignty
over different planets of this Universe'!
Thereby, creating apprehension on security
of entire World and the Universe, as a whole.

As merely a follower of humanity,
I also feel myself disturbed.
I do remember you in my distress to find-out
the light of guidance in darkness.
Let the concept of your idealism, as illustrated
in your 'Gitanjali', flourish once again
with new dimension on the world-forum.

08th May, 2016.

An Abandoned Buddha-Idol

In one full-moon evening–
while walking along a lonely road,
surprisingly I noticed a small idol,
resembling Lord-Buddha, in his meditation,
lying abandoned on a broken pedestal,
under an old banyan tree.

Though; the great soul of Lord-Buddha had
abandoned his body nearly two thousand
and five hundred years ago, I believe,
the sacred-souls of living-beings,
after leaving the body, do not exist in any form,
rather than through the memories.
Idols of great humanities evenly carry forward
those memories in this world, to motivate and
inspire human generations, in future.

The abandoned idol!
My mind didn't show any curiosity to find-out
the identity of that person, who had abandoned
you during the darkness, without anyone's notice.
Neither; I was interested to assess the gravity
of sins that person had committed.
Rather; I felt myself fortunate to locate
your presence in an isolated place.
Looking at elegance with luminous appearance

in a small-tiny shape, I could not resist inner call
of my soul, rather than to embrace you.
With passion I cleaned your dusty body-surface
with my apparels carefully, considering myself
lucky to be blessed with great fortune
by an invisible source of power.

Lord Buddha's idol!
Returning to my modest residence;
now I have placed you in an index on simple
but nicely decorated shelf, where many other
artistic and holy-figures are preserved.
Thereafter; with curious mind, I have turned
the page of a calendar, to find-out the day,
and significance of this date, if any.

To my great pleasure I find, this date is marked
as a holiday on the occasion of 'Buddha-Jayanti',
or holy birth anniversary of 'Lord-Buddha'.
The devotees believe; this date is celebrated as
the day of his enlightenment and also the date
of attaining salvation of his soul, as well.

Lord Buddha!
The unknown person; who had abandoned
your idol, perhaps has already acquired
a new one, by this time.
Abandonment of your idol by an unknown
has ultimately made me positive.
I feel myself blessed with an unexpected
and godly-gift as a process of purification

of my soul.
Your idol has ultimately inspired and
motivated my soul towards your teaching–
'Love ultimately wins over the hatred'.

In this process; I have realized–
'Love' is the purest form and gist of all faiths,
irrespective of any cast, class and creed.
From core of my heart, I pray to the memories
of all Religious Lords–
For the sake of lasting peace in this world
and safety of all planets in the universe,
please bless, enlighten and teach the mankind
to be liberal not only to one individual-faith,
but to all the faiths, for ultimate attainment.

21st May, 2016.

Drops of Tears on Withered Flowers

It is an early morning of rainy season.
Cheerful clouds; while floating over the sky,
are creating impressive-forms, keeping space
with the birds flying for unknown destination.

Passing through a dry spell of hot Summer,
soil at every corner of this park is eager
to get further greener.
I am a regular visitor to this park and familiar
to all the plants, saplings and creepers.
They consider me as one of their well-wishers.

This morning; while walking on the tracks,
passing through rows of decorative foliage,
I have noticed a bunch of depressed and
withered flowers, lying scattered on a red-stone,
the sitting slab for walkers, at a remote corner.
Further; I feel surprised to identify
a few drops of tears, side by the flowers, yet wet,
waiting for gentle touch of morning-Sun to dry.

I can very well recall, this stone-slab
is being occupied by a girl and a boy
of their teens regularly in the evening.
Now even; I can smell the presence of those
two young hearts, though they aren't visible

now anywhere nearby.
My mind feels scared to think and imagine
the probable sequence of last evening; reasons
and significances behind the drops of tears,
very close to those scattered flower-petals.
Last evening; was there any point of
misunderstanding or tussle in between
those two tender and young hearts?
My depressed mind goes on guessing and tries
to find out a probable possibility to reconcile
the difference, if grew up any in between those
two young minds and hearts.

I gently appeals to the gardener of the park
not to remove those withered flowers
from the stone-slab, also I decide to return
here again in the evening with a hope to meet
those young boy and the girl, who will come
to this park in the evening with bunch of
fresh flowers on their hands.

Let them remove these stale flower-petals
of last evening, and the misunderstandings
from their mind, if any!
In this rainy season all the plants and saplings
of this garden will be joyous in mind.

04th July, 2016.

The Mystique Memory

Out of my curiosity; at an importunate time,
I ask my queries to the most powerful figure
who is known as 'Life'–
What are the fundamental properties and
strategies being adopted to manage such
massive activities throughout the World,
from the time immemorial?

On every occasion; with an affectionate smile
my dearest, the 'Life' replies to my queries–
'The important part of the feedback
is being extended and furnished
by my reliable and trusted source,
who is known as 'Memory'.
With her great hypnotizing capacity;
I have convinced all human-beings
in the world to become obedient to me.
She has even taught me the lesson
more in details that, no one is free
from her clutch, which is specifically
known as the magical remembrance.'

Thereafter; since all my queries are answered,
respectfully, I give up my argumentative nature.
I bow my head to his lotus-feet and also offer
my soul to the 'Life' forever, till my last breath.

04th Sep, 2016.
Kolkata-9.

To be First Pedestrian at Dawn

At dawn; to explore virgin beauty of the Nature,
I come out of my hut alone, as a first pedestrian.
Following the muddy and zigzag road; I proceed
towards the ridge in between the green field
and find the activity of the field-mice and their skills
to make the holes passionately for their safe livings.
In addition to these; I witness the game, hide-n-sick
between the mongoose and the poisonous snake.

I bear great hope in my mind and find abundance of
dewy pearl-drops are shining rays of tender sunlight.
My mind is anxious to listen the euphonic rehearsal
of musical mode 'Voirobi' tune of gentle autumnal
airflow that awakens the dreamy birds in deep sleeps
along with their cheeks, in peaceful nests on the trees.
The blooming sunflowers with smiling petals,
while swinging in rhythm, beacon me for gossips.

On my return journey; the curious breeze enquires–
Have you been able to explore the secret of Nature,
or, to trace out any secret of the hidden treasures?

With bounty of pleasure; I disclose my mind,
and offer my both heart and soul, like a basket
full of assets with full of my mental satisfaction.
Further; graciously I answer–

I have gained all these from the generous Nature.
These assets will surely boost-up my mind greatly
to become a pedestrian with full of confidence
to walk a long distance in life, I have yet to cover.

28th October, 2016.

Tragedy—The Touchstone

Let my fate strike me with tragedy,
not only once, but again and again,
in order to enhance my power to sustain.

Oh my Lord of Fortune!
So far I am concerned; one human-being,
without having the feelings of tragedy
once at least, during his or her lifetime,
hardly gets the exposures thoroughly
to the peculiar and multifarious behaviour
of this earthly world and the nature.

It is my earnest appeal to the fate –
either to ignore or forget the tragic memory
of that fateful day, a holiday morning
of Autumn, the festive season!
We, the both, had already planned together,
a day before, to go to the temple,
with handful of flowers to offer a prayer.
My beloved; all of a sudden, left this world
untimely to an unknown destination even
against her will, leaving me alone!

Keeping aside your all the doubts;
hereby, I appeal to your kind consideration
that, I have come across all the odds and

tried hard to forget the tragedy in life and
become stronger than before.
Therefore; to make me more courageous
and stronger, please do not think twice
to offer any more tragedy to appear in my life,
till I get the final call, what so ever.

I shall remain grateful to your kindness again,
as you had favoured me earlier that had acted
like a 'touchstone' in my life, to lead me
towards the purity forever.

13th Nov, 2016.

Sensitivity of Demonetization

Poetry. Very well she knows the fact–
that, she is always close to my heart.
But, I could not call her for last few days.
Last night; she appeared in my dream
to realize actual reasons of my absence.
She looked a little bit upset, presuming
I am avoiding her on some flimsy pretext.

Politely I narrated her about the telecast,
that kept me busy to stand in a long queue
of hundreds of common people, outside the
bank-premises, near to my residence.
'High-value currency notes; presently
in circulation in the country, will be
invalid and treated as waste-papers,
unless those notes are exchanged
from the treasury, or approved outlets
within the stipulated time and date.'

Nearly a fortnight back; this sensational,
late-evening declaration by head of the State,
forced billions of citizens, wherever they are,
to spend their sleepless nights.
Early morning; people, like me, leaving aside
their regular duties, stood in long queue,
within no time, formed like an unending flow

of the river Ganges from Himalayan ranges
to the planes of different states in the country.

My dear lovely Poetry!
—It was irony of the day; like me, they had to
stand whole day in the open, till evening,
without any refreshment, even most of them
had to return empty handed at the end.
The incident followed repeatedly, day after
day, due to short-supply of new currency for
replenishment to public distribution system.

The query has been cropped-up in the mind
of general public; in a democratic set up,
whether the imposition of any such restriction,
without proper preparation, will not be
considered as violation of human-rights,
thereby, imposing physical punishment?

Ultimately; common people lost the patience,
expressed their arrogance, they were brutally
beaten-up by law-enforcing, security agencies.

The unarmed people, instead of currencies,
received bloody injuries, in spite of having
their legitimate cash-deposits.
Unfortunately; till date, dozens of people
died, living behind their dependents to suffer.

My dear Poetry!
Surely you will feel depressed to know the fact;

as reported that, demonetization has caused
cash-crunch and fuelled unemployment
for daily-wage labours in cities and rural areas.
Thereby; facing difficulties to survive,
and to feed their family members, many of
adult-male family-heads, in certain areas,
have ultimately approached a few hospitals,
duly approved, to go for vasectomy-operations,
with a hope to receive one-time cash-stipend
from the authorities, for family planning.

Winter parliamentary-session is supposed
to be commenced very shortly.
Entire opposition-leaders have united
to place a motion in the house for an unusual
explanatory reply, so as to decide –
who will be responsible for untimely death
of so many citizens of the country, while
they had been in queue to exercise their
basic human-right to collect the exchange,
out of their legitimate deposits.
– Are they not crusaders of democracy and
prey to administrative-failures of ruling party
of a democratic Nation?
– Are they not martyrs like soldiers, who are
protecting the Nation in the border areas?

My dear Poetry!
Very shortly; in my next communication,
I shall let you know the consequences
of demonetization that has caused miseries

to the common people, as the affluent-classes are free from queues, all over the nation. Hope; you will realize the touchy sentiments over these types of sufferings of the masses, and the reason, why I couldn't get in touch with you during these days, and to excuse me please!

24th Nov, 2016. Rohini, New Delhi.
The news, 'Demonetization of high-value-Notes' was announced on 08th November, 2016, at 8pm.

Bhopal Gas Tragedy

At the evening of Second December;
not a few, but uncountable numbers of idols
were incarnated for the worship
on the next day early morning.
On that shivering night; thousands of worshipers
were counting the moments in patience and waiting
for the morning of tender sunlight all over the sky.
The moonlight curiously came down to the slums
and dwelling units near the factory compound;
and peeped into the windows to enquire about the
welfare of every residents of the factory colony.

The status of the factory workers were either
the daily wage earners, or from the salaried class.
Last night; before going to their beds, all of them
had the dream of a new sunny and festive morning.
After attending to hard work throughout the day;
they were in deep sleep, happily embracing either
with their loving affectionate, or the life-partner.

The pregnant wife lovingly cautioned her husband–
My dear! The foetus I am carrying in my womb,
very often gives me the indication of movements
in this silent but cold and lengthy winter midnight.

Even; at dead of the night, the couple listened
the rhythmic musical sound of popular folk-song,
being sung by their neighbours in chorus, sitting
under the old banyan tree on the nearby courtyard.
The resonance of musical instruments-Tambourine
echoed all over the open air around the compound.

After a while; without anybody's knowledge;
the flow of poisonous gas-fumes blew up
from chimneys placed within the factory compound,
and gradually grabbed the atmosphere, like a monster.
The poisonous gas-fumes overpowered and polluted
the fresh air all around, thereby, creating suffocation
to inhale for all the living-beings around the locality.

In search of fresh air; the nocturnal owls were scared
and started flying with frustration in the dark sky.
Beaks of the pet parrot within the nice looking cage;
hanging on the balcony cried helplessly and ultimately
became silent without making any sound of babble.
Her green wings were still flapping for the breath.

The infant child became tranquil in suffocation
and was not even able to suck mother's breasts.
After a while; the wailing mother stopped breathing,
still embracing her deed child lovingly in her arms.

Even the foetus in mother's womb stopped palpitation.
The hue and cry from all directions broke the silence

of the cold midnight, and the resonance of folk-songs
turned into pathetic mourning that echoed all over,
beyond the boundary, or any other barrier.

Alas! Next morning; who would conduct the rituals
and offer prayers for incarnation of the idols, since
all living gods and goddesses had already turned to
merely lifeless idols, like the earthen models.
Innumerable habitats of Bhopal town, who had lived
merely hand to mouth turned into heaps of lifeless.
Even there was no trace of any relatives or siblings
to perform last rights and rituals of the dead bodies.
They all had been the sacrificed even before the day
the holy soul was born, the Twenty Fifth December.

The Progressive Human Civilization!
My dear! It was not the nature's obsession;
but a worst example of human negligence!
Perhaps; till date, the incident, the deaths of innocence,
stands as the most tragic example of industrial mishap!

My dear! You are the eternal force of the mankind,
who are still living as vibrant witness on this Earth.
If no one cares to remember those unfortunate souls
who lost their lives untimely by suffocation due to
leakage of poisonous gas from the factory premises
on fateful night-3rd December, Nineteen Eighty Four,
even if, no one bears the feelings of mourning for their

plaintive departure untimely from this earthy surface,
you, as the most sensitive witness, kindly observe
silence for a moment on their tragic remembrance
at the midnight of the same day, every year.

03rd December, 2016.

(In memory of those, who lost their lives due to leakage of lethal Methyl-isocyanate from a pesticide plant in Bhopal of MP-State in India, on the night of 23rd December,1984, and maiming thousands of lives.)

The Teary-Eyes

My dear 'Teary Eyes'!
Throughout the world, you are very popular.
Now a days, very rarely you remember me.
Perhaps; with an impression that, having
coming across many ups-n-downs in life,
I have already exhausted my precious treasure,
the tears, that the great Nature had gifted me,
while I was born on this holy Earth.

Earlier; when I was young, under teens,
very frequently, you appeared before me,
even without caring my sentiment, when
I had been enjoying delightful moments
with my well-wishers on happy occasions.

Gradually; I developed affairs with your
gracious behaviour, and vise-versa.
Very well I remember; out of my goodness,
you had sometimes taken the advantages
unaccounted, without caring my sentiments.

Even though; I had tried to my level-best
not to dishearten others, by any means.
But; hardly you bothered to console me
on those moments when I was drowned
in distress and suppressed under deep woes
on different tragic incidents.

By virtue of our cordial relationship
for such a long period in life; will you kindly
ensure me whether my well-wishers will shade
a few drops of their tears at the time when I shall
salute the world and address 'good-bye' to the Nature,
my well-wishers to proceed on my last journey
in response to the silent call of the Supreme,
for fulfillment of ultimate desire of salvation
of my soul?

Please inform them, in advance, to retain
and preserve their precious treasures, at least,
a few drops of tears, on my memory at last!

12th Dec, 2016.

An Amiable Straight-Line

Within my cripple-capacity of creativity;
shallow knowledge and meager intelligence,
I have not been able to assess the dynamism
of your shape and form, that is always
free from all angularities and curvatures
in character, status and formation.

In theoretical definition and in practice;
you are regarded as a mark of straightness
within the sphere of geometrical mathematics
and related applications only.
Therefore; your importance is unparallel and
absolutely unavoidable on any progressive
human project-implementations in the world.

Highly regarded intelligentsia
in social order have taught me a lesson—
The versatile expression of life;
throughout the Nature, is revealed always
in the angular shapes and forms.
Angularity and curvature reflects sobriety
and tenderness, as well as liveliness.
But; one straight-line never does the same.

For long; I have failed to understand the fact
and status of your straightness that reflects

firmness, stability and inspiration one needs
to move towards a high destination.
In this direction you mobilize yourself
on one's mind as stepping-stone to achieve
the success in human life.

Nevertheless; you are acknowledged
and regarded as the 'First-Lesson'
for basic education for every tender mind
to manifest inherent quality of intelligence,
already in man by birth, towards perfection.

I beg to offer my reaction–
On medical perspective; while going through
the report of electro-cardiogram, the flow
of blood in my ailing-heart in a straight-line
would mean an alarming sign of one's life,
as well as prior indication of ultimate call
for salvation, which is the earnest desire
of every mankind.

Bearing this desire in my mind,
I wish to offer my gratitude to a straight-line.
It is a well-known factor, none can ignore–
The mind, simple and straight by nature,
achieves the spiritual goal faster.

23rd Dec, 2016.
The poem is dedicated to the memory of my mother, who expired on this date in 2003.

Memoir of a Telephone-Index

Merely I am an insipid, Telephone-Index.
Today even; I can vividly remember–
To celebrate and welcome the 'New Year',
as trustworthy gift, I was happily presented
to my present master by one of his well-wishers.

Since then; all the time, I have been trying
to be loyal to my master, lingering the bond
with each other, every now and then.
Further; as one of his faithful companions,
always I have been trying to widen-up
his known circle by carrying all the names
and addresses alphabetically on the pages,
one by one, years after years.

I know very well; perhaps, at present
some of the names and addresses on my pages
might have lost the importance and relevance.
Some of them are even beyond recognition
and out of reach, of my master for connection.

I can feel the touchy moment and sentiments
of my master, when he dials to his close and
distant relatives and also associates, to know
their state of affairs and welfares.
Anxiously he waits for their reply and response

from other-end of the telephone calls.
And silently I observe the situation.
After a while; the response from other end
socks me even to listen–
'Sorry! The person you are calling and waiting
for reply, he or she is no more in this World
to respond to your anxious and gracious calls!

I notice sudden changes on my master's face
and keep myself idle and mum with open pages,
jolted with so many numbers and addresses.
Tears drop down on the lines of writings
as a mark of homage to the departed souls,
who had been very close to my master's heart
and mind for so long!
On these tragic moments; to feel his sentiment
I keep myself mum like a silent spectator!

Many times; to avoid confusion in future,
I remind my master to delete the names and
other details of those contacts who have left
this world and attained their desired destination
of ultimate salvation, but my master's mind
feels reluctant to listen to my suggestions.

Perhaps, my beloved hardly believes–
I also bear the same senses and sentiments.
I am now quite aged and being unimportant
to the younger generations of human society

as they are accustomed with new technologies, such as mobile phones, combined with many more facilities.

As an elderly; I realize, a day is not far away, when I shall also be abandoned and forgotten.

10th January, 2017.

To Paint Your Portrait

This morning; with noble feelings,
I concentrate my mind to paint your portrait,
as a mark of my respect to your greatness.
With all sincerity; under my personal care
I arrange the set-up of my drawing studio –
the easel, canvas, palette, brushes and colours.

Devoting sufficient time on the painting;
ultimately I realize that, I have drawn,
in my subconscious mind, a self-portrait,
instead of yours, on the same canvas.
On realization of the setback; I repent myself
from within, and curse my spurious mind–
How to pay homage to your highly adorable
image on this holy occasion!

Is there anyone who can realize the status
of my inner feelings –
Why my mind very often propagates my
thinking-process to enhance my own image
to an undue prominence; even at a place,
which is thoroughly out of context!
I pray to my inner soul to enlighten my mind,
and guide me to understand the fact –
This is thoroughly unforgivable and offensive.

Although; always my inner mind inspires me
to become an artist, truly to my heart and soul.
On contrary; my mental instinct, very often
conspires my thinking to follow the process of
egoism, out of infatuation to a great instinct.

15th January, 2017.

The Supreme Invigilator

Since; no allegations or complains
have been filed against me, I have so far
not been convicted even once by any court
of law in the civil society.
Thereby, all my associates and well-wishers
consider me as a person of good moral.

Although; you have always advised me
to be honest and humble, now let me confess
my weaknesses and drawbacks.
I haven't been courageous and bold enough
to overcome those Six heinous provocations
aimed at me, throughout my life-span
by those invisible forces in disguise, so far.
I have been victimized and surrendered
to their evil conspiracies, again and again.
Truly, I am an accused to your court of law.
Also liable to be punished, as well.

I feel myself guilty and not to be free
from prevailing court of law in civic society,
since I suppressed the offences that I had
committed knowingly in my conscious mind.
Moreover; those have, so far, been kept secret
from my associates, well-wishers who barely
considered me as one of their trustworthy

and also they had faith on my overall honesty.

From core of my heart; I admit –
I am grateful to you, as I have been blessed
by your grace to the extent of my ability
and caliber, I deserve.
But, my unscrupulous desires and ambitions
did not have proper assessment.
Very often; I became out of bound,
even blunt-eyed to asses my inherent talent
beyond limitation.

My adorable dear! I admit–
You blessed me the sense of esthetics
and lyrical concepts in abundance.
But; due to lack of my sincerity and confidence,
I could not transform those qualities into reality.
You had blessed me with the artistic-senses
with keen observation-power.
Whenever I tried to paint your portrait on canvas,
standing with confidence before the easel,
with paints and brushes in my hand,
I have failed miserably to portray your soul.
Perhaps my drawing has become very ordinary,
similar to any other drawings, I painted so far.

Often you appear in my dream to advise me
to be frank and free in my behaviour.
But I lack the interest in following your advice.
Due to these reasons; number of times, I failed
to admit those offences, that I had committed,

and to rectify myself there on.
Instead; I have kept them secretly to my heart
to avoid the curses and punishments as per law,
in vogue and prevailing in the society.

Even; I do not have an idea of the punishment,
that you have kept reserved and pending for me,
to be enforced on the day of your final judgment.

The Supreme Invigilator!
Even though, I expect your kind consideration.
Will you please allow me a chance of extension
to confess all my offences and wrong-doings,
that I have committed so far?

If it is not permitted–
As lesson, please punish me with your iron-hand.
No doubt, it will be a great boon for rectification
and purification of my soul to attain salvation.

22nd January, 2017.
New Delhi-85, India.

Appeal for the Bond, not Barbed

The flock of Birds!
whenever you like; stretching your wings,
freely you fly high in boundless sky.
Once upon a time, you inspired human mind
to conquer your free and vast territory
through the aviation-technology.
Do you feel disturbed to hear a shocking news
that is hovering in air, throughout the world?

On pretext of safety and security of mankind;
in near future, the world will be barricaded
within several walls, one after another.
Therefore; even by mistake, you do not prefer
to take birth as human-beings on this Earth.

There is an unpredictable apprehension;
while transforming yourselves into human-life,
you may have to undergo through the changes
in your inherent character and behaviour.
There is possibility, you may lose your
original character and broad-outlook of mind.
Human-race; presently domiciled in the World,
will not allow you to live-in here with dignity.
I am afraid, perhaps in near future –
the boundless sky will also be cordoned-off
within several walls and invisible barricades.

For the time-being; you may not be worried
as you are quite free to fly in the sky
in any direction and destination you desire.

Very well I remember the fairy-tales that
I had gone through during my childhood days.
The story elaborated; the bird, as dependable
and trust-worthy messenger, stretching wings,
flying a long distance, from one country
to another, had delivered the letter, written
by the captive princess to her beloved –
the young prince of her neighbour-country,
urging him to rescue herself from the captivity.

Similarly; please pass-on and carry forward
my agony to the head of states of countries
in their respective capitals, where they are busy
in planning for constructing and erecting walls
of boundaries in between neighbour-countries,
as future measure of their safety and security.

Oh the birds, flying high in boundless sky!
Being human-being of Twenty-first century
on this Earth, one may feel himself or herself
fortunate and claims to be progressive.
Thereby; transforming the earth-surface
polluted and merely suffocated.
Further; someone may feel himself proud
as owner of latest power, based on scientific
and technological development.
But in true sense; human-beings have turned

themselves captive within shallow barricade
of narrow outlooks, filled with self-interests,
to be satisfied themselves as safe and secured.
They may boast of their inherent intelligence.
Oh the birds, flying high in boundless sky!
Till date; no such restriction is imposed
on your flying movement, and even by mistake,
do not opt for a choice of getting human life!

The Leaders, very often, move door to door
of the citizens, seeking vote of confidence
by promoting slogan of 'Nationalism' or,
patriotism to strengthen national-integrity.
But very rarely; one talks about promotion
of philanthropic-internationalism, to inculcate
amity and brotherhood among the nations.

Oh the birds, flying high in boundless sky!
Visualizing evil consequences of the future,
ultimately my perturbed and confused mind
is shaky to invite my childhood friend-'Poem'
to my simple and shabby compound.
With an aspiration of achieving influence
and power; please do not expect to get a boon
of achieving human-life on this Earth.
Otherwise; heavenly feelings of Sun-Moon
and Stars will automatically be out of bound
from your life, even forever!

Can you please sing the songs in such an
overwhelming tune, that will motivate your
mind to deplete or demolish the barricades
like the 'Berlin-Wall' to promote brotherhood
and national integrity beyond the borders?

27th January, 2017.

(Today's newspaper carries a report: recently elected US-President is in favour of erecting boundary-wall between Two countries- USA and Mexico.)

Spring abandons the Dry-leaves

Only a year back, during the last Spring–
Then; we, the tender leaves of trees were
at the centre of attraction on earthy surface.
The southern wind, bees and butterflies,
the flocks of birds, along with the Nature,
were pleased on our tender foliage beauty.

Earlier; we, the leaves used to compose
lyrics of murmurs to sing cradle-songs
to please newly born chicks in the nests
on the branches, while their parent-birds
were flying away, in search of their needs.
Day-by-day, the cheeks grew-up and
abandoned the nests to find their fate.

We witnessed the hot Summer.
And we became pleased and satisfied
to extend shed equally without any priority
to all the tired passersby who used to find
for a safe place to take temporary rest.

Thereafter; we welcomed the seasons–
Monsoon, Autumn, as well as cold Winter.
As we have lost the lively green effects
and turned into pale, the Nature has now
decided to abandon us forever.

The trees are even silent on this decision,
as a sign of their whole hearted acceptance
with an advance-assurance of blessings of
new leaves in ensuing Spring season.

On arrival of Spring; the Nature is blooming
all-around with new hopes and aspirations.
We are now abandoned on the grassy-ground
under trees by the same wind, who had once
been cordial to us on our formative period
as tender green foliage.

The Spring salutes the Sun every morning
to bring cheers for all, except us, and say
'good-bye' to departing souls, to focus on
the 'life-cycle', which is common for all
on this Earth, without an exception.

27th March, 2017.

Ardor of the Guava-Tree

In dancing mode; Robin, the restless tinny bird
flies on the branches of a green tender guava-tree,
and cheerfully whistles in the musical rhythm
to call her mate without rest in this early Spring.
The bird finds her mate, and the pair decides
to make their nest on a branch of the same tree
for living together and bringing-up their cheeks.

Witnessing this lovely sequence; the guava-tree
desires to be green further and bear juicy fruits.

The Spring is at the verge of passing on.
Stems of the branches; covered with green leaves,
are bloomed, like the teenaged bride, adorned
beautifully on the event of her marriage-function.

Sensing heartfelt desires of the blooming flowers;
for pollination, the guava-tree conveys to breeze air
to carry the essence and pass on goodwill messages
to the hornets, bees and butterflies without delays.

The guava-tree earnestly appeals to the Sun—
I wish to achieve ultimate fulfillment in my life.
Let all my stems bear the juicy fruits for others.
I am very eager to pollinate my blooming flowers
by all my lovers-- the hornets, bees and butterflies.

They are my playmates since my childhood days.
Please do not set; till my desires are fulfilled.
We all on the globe salute to your divine force.

16th April, 2017.

An Impudent Guest

Honestly speaking–
I am one of many impudent guests
on this boundless and generous Earth.

Whenever a guest steps-in at my tiny
modest residence, the visitor brings
either a bouquet, or, a bunch of flowers
of aromatic essence as a good gesture.
Otherwise; a tiny packet of sweets
or a modest gift, as a mark of souvenir
for the host and relatives.
Nonetheless; this practice is in vogue
worldwide almost in every civil society,
irrespective of status, class and creed.

On this generous Earth, on my own right,
I claim myself, as owner of the wealth,
in accordance with an individual capacity,
without going into the fact that –
whether, I really deserve to be the owner
of this property in any capacity!
Have I not occupied and forced my right
unethically on it, claiming the ownership?
And, without having legitimacy, I enjoy
all the facilities, beyond the generations!

In return; I have not, on single occasion,
expressed gratitude to the bona-fide and
original owner of this wealth, the great
and fabulous Earth!
Undoubtedly, I am a shameless-defaulter
and an impudent guest in every respect.

My dear Earth! Whenever and wherever;
in my known circle I discuss this vital issue,
I am always being shunted-out of the forum
and cursed as a worthless and fool.

03rd May, 2017.

Tantalization of the Spring

With my humble gesture; I enquired
from Spring, the king of all seasons–
Why he was displeased on me,
since his deceptive actions are still being
followed thereon!

Winter season has recently said 'Good-bye',
the Spring, king of all the season, is eager
to beautify the beloved Nature worldwide
with multicoloured foliage all over.
On his advice; mischief maker, the black-bird
'Koel', in his inherent musical tune, casually,
tries to remind me foregone tragic memory
that I had tried hard to forget and abandon.

Can anyone tell me his intension
behind these preplanned actions?
Can anyone please tell me, whether
any punishment is hanging on me
for the fault, that I had committed earlier,
or, any other mischievous behaviour?

Dear Spring! At the end of hectic day;
I was relaxing in deep sleep at night
and enjoying a melodious dream.

To comply your invisible instruction,
the Koel's compassionate and musical tune –
'Coo-hoo', 'Coo-hoo', utterly disillusioned
my dream instantly.

You were not unfamiliar of my aspiration.
All along; I had a desire in mind to be cordial
with the black bird, Cuckoo, or 'Koel'.
To overcome those tragic incidents of the past,
I cherished my dream to make a happy-nest
to spend the rest of my life with the 'Koel'.

But this is the irony, when the feeling of love
stared budding in core of my sensitive heart,
suddenly he disappeared, like a deceiver.
Avoiding heat of Summer-season, I looked
for him throughout the wild green.

The seasons— Monsoon, Autumn passed
one after another.
I had a hope; perhaps these seasons would be
kind enough and sympathetic to me, so that,
I would be able to overcome the sorrows.

Ultimately, the 'Time' taught the lesson,
that, I had mistaken to face the situation.

Spring, the tantalizer!
Perhaps; you were aware, the bird 'Koel',
the deceiver, has appeared again in this season
and is flying freely on the trees in my locality.

As usual; in his inherent heart-rending
musical tunes, he is singing to soften
my heart and mind.
Please tell him not to be so cordial to me.
My estranged mind will no longer be able
to bear his deceptive-behaviour, any further.

08th May, 2017.
The bird 'Cuckoo' is known as 'Koel',
or, 'Cockil' in South-Asian Countries.

When My Mind Feels Depressed

Even, with, or, without any valid reason,
when the mind feels depressed, I wish
to handover this Earth to the custody of Sun,
the most firebrand planet in the Universe,
and to observe minutely–
whether the Sun can change the behaviour
of this Earth, and rectify the attitude
of human-races on its surface, who are always
keen in implementing their inherent desire
of expansionism and to overpower others!

Alternatively; let the Sun engulf them entirely
into flames and destroy the life completely.
And thereafter–
what would be my status as an individual?
Invariably; I would be transformed into atoms,
floating around the limitless space, continuously.

Nonsense! It is nothing but an absurd concept.
Otherwise; with, or, without any valid reason,
when I am annoyed and disgusted with you,
I think–
No more living-together with you, rather to opt
for an exile, away from human-settlement, and
proceed towards the Nature, to be surrounded
with deep and green forestry.

There; gladly I may decide to spend the nights
in the nests of the birds.
I'll feel myself complacent to become familiar
with elegant fireflies of twinkle-lights.

But; following the given time meticulously,
as and when, you approach before me,
with a glass of water in one hand and daily-doses
of prescribed medicines on the other,
I get bygone memories back, the day I had lost
my mother forever!
Apparently; I look at the circular vermilion-dot
on your forehead, that resembles like rising Sun,
glows to enlighten my mind and heart.
Your posture, at this moment reminds me
as an elegant beauty of 'Ajanta' cave-painting.

19th May, 2017.

Appeal to all the Prophets

After taking a holy-dip in the river-Ganges;
while offering prayer to the morning-Sun,
silently I appeal to the prophets of all religions
to take birth on this Earth, once again,
to bring-back the feelings of harmony
in the heart and mind of present-day mankind
who are always on their heels to achieve
the supremacy over others by any means.

I am not sure; now-a-days, whether
the majority of human beings on this Earth,
pay respect to your lifelong devotions
and teachings for welfare of all living-beings.
But; I do offer my humble salute to the
selfless efforts and services, you rendered.

Will you please excuse me,
if I express my mind on your ultimate score?
The main objectives of your teachings
and preaching are, very often, being diverted
into different directions.
Instead of upholding human mind to become
broad-minded, it is indulging expansionism
in many other dimensions.
Instead of practicing forgiveness; the policy
of arrogance is being practiced, in order to

proclaim the power of supremacy over others.

Now; it is my humble appeal to you all,
kindly to take birth once again on this Earth,
as a mark of combined effort to be strong enough,
to change the mindset of present-day mankind
and ultimately to save the planet, Earth.

Please give a forceful clarion-call to all your
devotees and disciples to understand–
that; Religion and all the faiths are meant for
cultivating integrity, and not to disintegrate
the social fabrics of the society, worldwide.

Oh, the holy Souls!
Will you kindly respond to my hearty appeal?

22nd May, 2017.

Attitude of my Odious-Mind

All these have been possible
by virtue of their noble-hearted gestures.
But; till date, my odious-mind has been
reluctant to admit these hard facts.
My neighbours have encouraged me always
and very often praised my qualities.
On different occasions and number of times,
they have even felicitated me with laurels.
They do not bother for a moment that;
their patronage and support have applauded
an egoism within me, time and again.

The great and mighty 'Death',
in the recent past, served me an warrant,
although I felt, his visit was uncalled for.
In fact; I was then on my sick-bed
and completely unconscious due to Coma.
I failed to offer him a gracious reception
which he deserves always by all living-beings.
But; he didn't take offence even for a while.
Rather; his generosity granted me graze-time.

But my odious-attitude; till date, have failed
to appreciate the gentle-gesture, that has been
extended to me by different noble-hearted.

During that crucial moment; most of them,
who resisted the great 'Death' directly,
or indirectly to take me away, were neither
my friends, nor blood-relations.
Rather; unknown an auto-rickshaw-driver,
the guards and attendants of hospital staff,
the nurses and doctors, who extended their
noble-gestures of holy-services towards me
to come-out of the grievous situation.
Ultimately; with their various blessings,
I recovered and gained my life back again.

It is absolutely a godly-gift to me
by all of them and it has been ultimately
proved to be my second-birth on this Earth.
But; my odious-mind ignores to express
gratitude and appreciate the noble behaviour.
Moreover; it has all along been reluctant
to admit the time-tasted 'Truth'!

25th May, 217.

Mirth of Mustard Field

Crossing the boundary of our mud-hut;
beyond the courtyard, that is nicely coated
with clay-paste and also decorated with
different artistic and auspicious folk motifs,
let both of us walk down to the grassy ridge
in between the vast green mustard field
that is glowing with bright yellow flowers,
kissing tender Sun in presence of breeze air.

The flowering mustard plants
are gracefully enjoying the togetherness
of jovial bees and butterflies for pollination;
without caring the flocks of birds—
the naughty Parrots and querulous Martins.

When the Sun tilts towards the West,
and the dusk appears on the horizon,
the tiny petals of yellow flowers feel tired,
politely convey good-bye to bees and birds.

During the dusk; beyond human territory,
surrounded with green foliage all over,
in presence of vibrant Nature, I wish to offer
and spray handful of yellow Sun-rays
on your beautiful, unornamented slim figure
for a mirthful evening, Oh my dear!

27th May, 2017.

The Dominant Fisherman

The most tactful and dominant fisherman–
Easily influences everyone's heart and mind;
whomsoever he decides, and also can bring
that soul under his domain within a moment.
Further; even to trap human-beings, he expands
his magical fishing-nets worldwide quite neatly.
None can run away from his clutch and grips.

Covering a long passage of life;
now at my age, I have come to know the art
of different patterns of his fishing-nets that
trap different people, whomsoever he decides.
Some sets of nets are knitted of cotton-threads.
Some are made of nylon-stings, some are even
produced while following modern techniques.
And the nets are spread all over the world
in invisible fashion by this witty fisherman
to enchant or to hypnotize the mankind.

The fishing nets have many categories–
Anger and abuse, envy and hatred, fury-lust,
kidnap and killing, cruelty, theft and robbery,
outrage and rape, lavishness and luxury.
Some nets are also identified as –
Love and respect, worship and devotion,
service and sacrifice, lastly renouncement
and attainment.
It is an irony; till date I have not been able

to identify any kind of nets which are known
as rendering selfless-service for the needy
of the society, without having any kind of
expectation in return.
Rather; to fulfill any individual's desire
for name-fame and recognition thereon,
we conspire to manipulate the situation
in our favour under the catchy definition,
or, slogans as stunts, to convince others.

While passing through the daily life;
my mind very often realizes the fact that,
I have been unknowingly entangled within
the traps of his nets, and thereby feeling
myself suppressed and suffocated from within.

Diligently; I appeal to the invisible fisherman,
having enormous fatidic power, kindly to make
me now free from all these entangles,
in order to get the essence of 'Attainment'.
Although I know – even for a moment;
his highness hardly bothers to show leniency
of his command on me as an individual,
and on entire Universe as well.

Honestly! He is not at all amiable to me;
rather, an adamant and dominant fisherman
who has always confused me to place himself
safe and free from all his nets of conspiracy.

24th June, 2017.
Kolkata – 9.

My Avid Mind

While arranging the social functions;
the influential associates, known to me,
forget to include my name very casually
in their long lists of important invitees.

My avid mind anxiously awaits to receive
invitations from them; as my mind considers,
an invitation from them, will obviously
enhance my image and prestige in the society.
I linger on waiting, but all in vain!

The friends; who consider me as one of their
trustworthy well-wishers, invite me in time
and ask to grace the occasion by my presence.
Concluding the logic that, my presence
will surely grace the occasion and enhance
the prestige of the host and not this guest,
my avid mind swings between Yes and No!

The humble heart evaluates the fact–
Why the mind opposes to allow for my
physical presence to them, who cordially desire
my association from their both, mind and heart.
My avid mind; looking for gaining prestige,
hankers always for the invitation from them,
who do not bother and care me as their own.

06th July, 2017.

At That Moment

At midnight; while I am alone at home,
I listen humming of a pretty hornet, which
remains captive in a dark corner of my hut.

Sensing my loneliness; she, in her usual
emotional and submissive tune, appeals to me—
How long she will have to remain captive
in such suppressed and neglected condition!
When she will be allowed to transform her
inherent talents, lying idle so far, into
various musical rhythms, that might not only
bring appreciation, but also motivate and
inspire the world for experimental avenues!

She; with her diligence, further elaborates—
On that moment; she will obviously feel
a sense of freedom that might ultimately
lead her towards the perfection of her soul.
Moreover; she will be able to explore
the charisma of time-tasted truth, which is
so far lying suppressed and confined
at a dark corner of her heart and mind.

The cheerful hornet looks for that moment
to avail jovial opportunity while humming
every corners of my judicious soul.

08th August, 2017.

Void—Nowhere !

In my subconscious mind; once
a saintly soul appeared before me
in my dream and consoled me gently,
My child! Take it granted–
No space in the Earth, even a palace,
or a hut, even at an abandoned cave,
or, a deep cavity unapproachable
remains void, vacant or empty.

> Obviously; it is already filled-up
> either with air, or, by the insects,
> bats, birds, and the animals.
> If not; it might even be occupied
> by the people as unauthorized
> habitats, outnumbered dwellings.

Thereby; obviously it is better, if
it is occupied by a decent human-being,
having a positive sense of humanity
in mind and soul, all the time.
Now, it is high time to judge yourself–
in which category you really belong!
If decent; do not do the mistake,
or, hesitate to fill-up the void.

18th August, 2017.

Wailing of the Pigeon-couple

Mainly for our amiable behaviour;
neither the mother Earth, nor, the Nature ever
restricted to our movement in their vast domain.
While flying freely in the sky; we two pigeons
of bird-family became intimate with each other.
Thereafter; the intimacy developed into affair.

To materialize the hope and fulfill our desire;
we made a nest at a remote corner–
in-between the space of window-frame and
glass-pane of a flat, in a multistoried building
that we used to visit very often earlier, and
we thought, it would really be safe to lay eggs
and bring-up the chicks, since the residents
of the flat, mainly the kids used to offer us
food-grains and the left-over, as token of love
towards our amiable behaviour and gestures.

We really considered them as our
trustworthy-protectors and the well-wishers.
Time passed-on happily, the chicks were born
under our affectionate and parental-care.
We were grateful to the mighty Nature
for her abundant-blessings on us
to fulfill our ultimate aspiration and desire.

But alas! Perhaps; with the anticipation
of unwarranted noise, dirtiness and nuisance
yet to be created by the new-born chicks,
in one evening, the resident, without our notice,
pushed-down our loving-nest to clean the space.
All of a sudden, our infants faced instant death!

Never we expected this kind of harsh-treatment
from human-beings, who always recognize
and honour the pigeons of winged-family as
'Messenger of Peace' worldwide!
Now we realize–
It is not the love and affection bestowed on us.
But; merely the publicity-stunts by the
crazy human-beings to enhance their images
on different public-forums, time and again!

Though; we are the bereaved-parents
of innocent-chicks, we sincerely pray for peace,
prosperity and happiness for the mankind.

25th November, 2017.

Glow of a Dismissal-Letter

Today even; I preserve the dismissal-letter
that was issued to me several decades back.
I salute to those bosses who had formulated
that hard decision against me from behind.
'Your service is no longer required'–
The wordings of that letter repeated
even in my dream, time and again!

The phenomenon of that event–
as I recount today, had really forced me
to proceed to an unknown destination.
That dismissal-letter; though initially
disappointed my heart and mind severely,
in other way, it had consoled and signaled
a faint beam of light on the other end
of a narrow and dark tunnel, where I was
walking alone, and reminded me the proverb,
–'failure is the pillar of success'.

That had no doubt; guided me to generate
sufficient courage, and stamina for struggle,
power of conviction as well, to prove my
inherent mettle at every crucial points in life.
That had grown the perseverance within me

and had brought the source of success
that had ultimately offered me the prestige,
laurels and dignity in the society.

In the afternoon; as I plan for my retirement,
I bring-off those hidden treasures one by one,
and kiss that dismissal-letter with loving care.
That letter had turned into pale in appearance,
but the lines of wordings still glow like spark
of lightening as inspiration for next generation.

In late evening; now I am waiting to listen
those wordings once again from none other than
the most dynamic, invisible but mighty force,
who regulates earthly life-cycles for all beings.

28th January, 2018.

Humming of an Unwanted Hornet

The presence of Winter is not yet over.
This morning; my mind is keen to find-out
new themes on Nature's reflection to write
a poem, or to draw the painting.
For successful implementation of new ideas;
deliberately I keep myself captive in a room,
shutting its door and the glass-windowpanes
from inside, to get minute concentration.

I find, a restless hornet flying around
outer surface of the glass-pane to find an
entry-point into this room.
To avoid probable disturbance, I open-up
silently a part of the window to drive away
the unwanted tiny guest, who appears to me
like a flying messenger to my address.

This tiny insect; like a little girl of her teens,
creates musical sound in its flying wings.
At once; I realize inner meaning of its humming,
– "Guy! Sitting comfortably in a captivity;
away from elegant Nature, it is merely a
futile venture on your part to prove yourself
as a poet of extra ordinary merit and caliber.

Now; 'Spring', the king of all the seasons,
is blooming around, and the Nature is glowing
in several shades of colours of vibrant grace.
Allover; gentle breeze is flowing fragrances
of seasonal flowers to rejuvenate human mind.

Do not lag behind to listen devotional songs
being offered in the form of morning-prayers
by the Cuckoos to please the elegant Spring.
Dear! Life is mortal; therefore, do not deprive
your fortune from availing this opportunity
deliberately by locking yourself in captivity."

01st March, 2018.

Yearning to become a Firefly

Let the Sun and the Earth settle their
disputes on equation of the solar energy.
Do not let the jolly weaving-birds
and the tiny fireflies bother themselves
on this critical issue, and not to hamper
their cordial relation in between,
on these points,
– as; when the Sun will illuminate
  one surface of this Earth to bring
  a new morning, and which part will
  be plunged into darkness, in absence
  of sunlight, to determine the night.

My dear mother Nature!
During night; the stars, above the sky,
feel shy to illuminate the vast greenery
down to the Earth, and in this situation,
only the tiny fireflies come forward
to twinkle the nests of weaving-birds,
hanging high from the tall palm-trees.

Nature! My dear Mother!
  So far; I have not yet been able to do
  anything worth to your satisfaction,
  either directly, or, indirectly.
  Sincerely; I yearn to be a tiny firefly.

With your blessing; let me twinkle the spark
of light, even for a while, to the dark areas,
where the Sun has ever neglected to shine.
With my limited capacity, let me glow
the nests of tiny weaving-birds at night.

> Let the mother-bird feel satisfaction
> to yield affection to her gawky-chicks,
> or even to spark like twinkle lights to an
> ignorant person for a vision of knowledge.

In real sense; I shall be delighted and feel
satisfied to carry out a few responsibilities
in order to justify my honourable deputation
to this World for a noble cause, even a little,
only for a while.

05th March, 218.

Role of Truth & Deceit in Life

Having been brought-up within the Heart,
under motherly care of gracious Mind,
the confused 'Egoism' is yet to decide,
whom to revere and who should be friendly
to the Soul– either the 'Truth' or the 'Deceit!'

By virtue of growing age; Egoism has realized,
that the 'Truth', though being considered as
minority-force in the society, is not really eager
to win the respect of the masses.
It believes, the final outcome will be decided
at the last stage of life, as it had happened
on holy occasion of 'last-supper' in the 'Bible'!
Or, during last-journey of the prince Yudhistir
in Hindu-epic, 'Mahabharata'!

Since the defeat is never acceptable;
the adamant 'Deceit' declares,
–'The World celebrates applause in my favour.
Even the administration on ruling-front, and
judiciary in the society largely remain busy
in settling on my multifarious activities.
And the history puts all these in records!'

Experiencing the ups and downs in life;
now my Heart and Mind conclude,

—'On the day of final judgment, the 'Truth',
representative of the minority is enthroned
and crowned to discharge the responsibility
as Supreme-Judge.

The demoralized ' Deceit', already plunged
into disarray, remains silent before the bench
at the moment of declaring final judgment
by the honourable Juries.

21st March, 2018.

Ideal Ruling—The Tree of Wisdom

While getting birth in this Earth,
human-beings are blessed with two eyes
by the kind-hearted Nature.
The reason– though we can possibly see
in one eye; but the vision through two eyes
together felicitates to perceive the depth and
dimension of a viewing object distinctly.
In fact; the combined efforts of both eyes
are absolutely imperative to achieve
the benefits of Nature's generous gifts.

From very beginning of human evolution
'Repression', as well as 'Reformation'
are co-existing side by side on this Earth.
Phenomenon of these two are contradictory
and hostile to each other all the time.
The rivalry between these two continues
either openly, or flows like as undercurrent.
In human mind these two concepts grow
silently like tender saplings; and gradually
with passage of time, turn to deep-rooted plants.
One may be identified as a 'Plant of Poison'.
The second one may be identified as
'Tree of Wisdom', providing shelters to needy.

On the perspective of vast political-scenario;
worldwide, according to intellectual-analogy,
these two characteristics are classified either
as 'Capitalism', or 'Socialism' to some extent.

To Rule, or being ruled over through the process
of any one of these two 'ism', or 'ideology'
might prove to look at an aspect in one eye only.
Through passage of time; evaluation has been
carried out to assess the effect of positivity
and negativity of both the systems on society.
This process may be called as 'Reformation'.

Like many others; I have also come across
the nations, where 'Autocracy' is in ruling-front.
I have even witnessed the effect of 'Capitalism'
on liberal societies.
I have come across the nations, where citizens
are governed by the regulations of 'Socialism'.
Further; I have also witnessed the effects
of actions initiated by the followers of religious
'Fanaticism' in power.

Let the researchers of 'Political-Science' burn
their midnight-oil to find out a new theory, or,
to invent an 'ism', which can possibly drive out,
or, eliminate all the ill-effects, which have been
generated so far in the society out of Autocracy-
Capitalism-Socialism, even the Fundamentalism,

Fanaticism in vogue, also can achieve
rational development with minimum side-effects
like exploitations, thereby, leaving aside these
geographical boundaries on this Earth.

A public gathering eagerly enquires to me –
The Poet! Please suggest the remedial steps
to be followed to overcome the exploitations
which are going on, in the society for ages.

In response; politely I answer–
My dear friends! Take it granted that I am not
an expert of Social or Political-Science.
Please do not take offence on my comments.
Do not convict me if I am proved wrong.
I believe; implementation of any one of these 'ism'
meticulously to rule-over the country is considered
likely to perceive a vision only through one eye.
And; not through two eyes as we are blessed with.
Every policy needs to be seen through two eyes
before it is implemented for action.
That means to consider the points of 'Reformation',
in order to neutralize the bad effects which are being
originated out of following any one of these 'isms'.

I strongly believe; only 'Exploitation'
for safe-governance, or, 'Reformation'
indicating implementation so called liberal policy
for ruling, may not be capable of achieving
all round welfare of human-beings in the society.
Individually; any of these policies may not be

able to provide permanent solution
in the line of social reformation for any Nation.
Balanced implementation of both the two;
such as exploitation along with 'Reformation'
can pave the path of all round prosperity
of the common people.
Both the two are complimentary to each other
towards fulfilling the very objectives of the life.
Exercising the power of administration,
coupled with rational and logical exploitation,
as well as introducing reformation on social norms
may show the light of a new horizon for prosperity
and enhancement of human dignity.

Always I admit–
Continuous exploitation of human right
by a section of people in power is not desirable.
Similarly; evading the responsibility or avoiding
accountability may bring the downfall and
massive devastation on national development
of any Nation.
One can remember the past instances;
the World has come across, one after another.
Similarly, only a bunch of prospective reformation
without proper execution may not ensure the growth
to bring tangible prosperity for future generation.

In conclusion; I believe in perceiving a vision
through both the eyes, instead of only one.
To get an image of reflection; as well as refraction,
I am in favour of implementing a liberalized policy

with logical and realistic approach.
Accordingly; to follow the process of 'Capitalism' in totality, without taking into account of positive points of 'Socialism', may prove a failure to achieve ultimate success for overall prosperity of the common people.

Balanced adaption of both the ideologies in life ultimately paves path towards all round prosperity in human life, thereby, extends solution like an ideal ruling–'The Tree of Wisdom'.

28th March, 2018.

'Koel' narrates fear of the Forest

At the end of the Spring; and beginning
of the Summer season, in this early morning,
the pretty bird 'Koel' has awakened me,
while singing in her usual melodious and
enchanting tune –'Koo-hoo', 'Koo-hoo',
to wish me the New year greetings.

During her practice; at an opportune time,
curiously I address my queries,
– Please educate me on the main reason
of your melodious but plaintive tune
that impresses the mind of every human
at every corner, throughout the world.

With great patience and enthusiasm; I wait
for her answer to enlighten me there on.
At an appropriate interval, politely the 'Koel'
responds,
– Dear! You all know, music is my prayer
and holy devotion to Nature, the Supreme.
Today; through my prayer, I try to endorse
my inner feelings of anguish and pains
of the green foliages all around, which are
in great danger to sustain their existences
on this vast earthy surface.

The pretty bird further continues,
–My dear well-wishers! For last several years,
during the Spring, I, along with other birds,
do visit this locality regularly to offer our

musical melody, to please your neighbours.
More precisely; you will be knowing the fact
that, the full-grown 'Krishna-Chuda' tree
which bloomed red-flowers gorgeously
during the Spring to aspire us, and also to
beautify your locality, used to extend us
its cordial hospitality whole heartedly.

–Unfortunately; during this Spring season,
we have failed to locate that ill-fated tree
and shocked to see its uprooted and
dismembered trunk, duly cut into pieces,
and heaped at a corner in your locality.
And; this is the irony to note, that space
has been occupied to construct a high-rise,
housing complex for human settlement.

–Now, my friend! Please tell me,
in such a tragic situation, how I can sing
in joyous tune, instead of punitive mood!

–My dear beloved listeners!
You all love our songs in rhythmic tune.
The green forest and vast foliages
do love us, and all the birds too.
Now; how we can sing in joyous and
melodious tune after this catastrophe,
losing our beloved companion for ages,
that very 'Krishna-Chuda', the loving tree
of Lord-Krishna, the almighty!

15th April, 2018. Rohini, New Delhi.
** The bird 'Cuckoo' is also known as 'Koel'*
or 'Kokil' in South-East Asian Countries.
The tree 'Krishna-Chuda' is the local term
of 'Caesalpinia-Pulcherrima'

An appeal to all Individuals

The cobalt-blue sky on the boundless space
of the Universe passionately displays
twinkle-stars, along with other elegant planets,
far and near from each others.
The sky; like tiny human toddlers, plays
hide and seek with floating clouds.
Also paints the rainbow with masterly strokes
in marvelous colours, covering the horizon.
A holy dot of bright vermilion, known as Sun,
always glares on her wide forehead.
On her dark curly-wavy hair there illuminates
the most enchanting jewel known as Moon.

Human toddlers on their mothers' laps,
down the Earth, cordially beckon her
with romantic and inquisitive notes
during evening while listening cradle-songs.
The Moon, while flowing with the clouds
still looks down to her innocent playmates.

On such a majestic and vibrant sky—
A few biased and power-crazy members
of human race have taken evil-oath to destroy
her virginity for ultimate exploitation of its
untapped natural resources; under the slogan
of scientific exploration and invention.

Is it not a cowardly act on their part to prove
the supremacy on their other neighbours?

My dear sensible citizens!
Following the process of vanity and egoism;
one can never find an avenue of solution
to find peace and prosperity of humanity,
in order to attain ultimate salvation of souls.
Instead; kindly give-up this greedy conspiracy
to claim supremacy, self-glorification of vanity.
Rather; live and let this beautiful World and
the Universe live together, along with us.

By following this noble act on your part,
you will surely enlighten human mind and heart.
It will create a new luminary in entire space.
The generations yet to come on world-surface
will find a luminous precedence as a mark of
their future inspiration and guidance.

23rd April, 2018. World Book Day.

Not Divided, But United India

While declaring Independence of our Nation;
it was divided, but not on the basis of public-opinion!
Subservient for generation; the citizens desired
to achieve independence of their holy motherland.

At that time; the citizens had no other option
but to assent to the verbal assurance given
by the leaders who were enjoying power.

On pretext of partition; their main intension was
to hold the power in their favour that had ultimately
compelled large section of citizens to abandon their
ancestors' homeland and become refugee.

The citizens have been facing severe repression,
riots-war-continuous border conflicts and killings
of neighbourly siblings-cousins now even !
Much needed peace-prosperity and happiness
have ultimately been banished indefinitely.

One by one; more than Seven decades passed on.
But; the assurance did not yield the ultimate result.
The public-grudges are being reverberated–

The citizens! Now utter a clarion call.
We do not accept the partition of our homeland
and refuse to honour any such understanding.

Let us get back the same undivided motherland, India
where, on earlier days, there was no discrepancy
of cast-class-creed-language and individual identity.

We all are the children of one mother-'India'.
And we demand to get back peace-prosperity
and cordiality which were followed by our
ancestors, generations after generations.

We all are children of those followers who used to
consider this undivided land as their sacred Nation,
namely the 'Mother India'.

16th December, 219.

(In view of public-resentment against recent alteration of the 'Citizenship Amendment Act'.)